It's All About

CHOICE

Testimonials

It's All About Choice is a book for everyone. Even though it demonstrates the love and courage we all must have to help save the foster child, it is also about the choices all families make every day.

Susan Gilgenbach
Mother - Secretary

After having read *It's All About Choice* and practiced law in excess of 35 years, I find it an eye opening and innovative approach to solving many of our juvenile problems. This book is a must read for today's social worker, and all judges and attorneys who deal in these areas!

C. Thomas Kier
Attorney and Counselor at Law

"Open my eyes O' Lord." Having never wanted to sit on the sidelines and not get in the game, this simple prayer, 'open my eyes Lord', brought me into the battle. In becoming a youth pastor and a father of an adopted child, God opened my eyes to the evil that surrounds us all.

Delbert hits this right on the head in his book; the battles that are going on around us, but people won't open their eyes to it. They feel right at home on the sidelines. Even worse are the ones fighting on the 'other' team. Delbert took the sight God gave him and entered the battle, and there are many stories of his battles and victories here in this book. All in the name of Jesus!

Greg Woolf
Youth Pastor, Teacher, and Football Coach

hope
faith
live
believe
dream
love
laugh
trust

It's All About
CHOICE

delbert harvey
with **barbara silliman**

ISBN 978-0-9

Table of Contents

It's All About
CHOICE

Forward

If intrigue, mystery, and story twists grab your attention, you will eagerly read each and every page of this book. Our story is akin to the old historical fiction *The Man without a Country*, published in 1863 in the *Atlantic Monthly* by Edward Everett Hale.

In The Man without a Country, Philip Nolan is convicted of treason and sentenced to live the rest of his life as a prisoner on the high seas. He must never touch land or see home again. The story describes the intense loneliness, pain, and depression that plague Nolan as he travels to nowhere.

Our story is like that. It is about the 'little people' in America who are sentenced to the foster care system. These 'little people,' 127,000 of them, are destined to bounce from house to house, never finding a home. Loneliness, pain, and depression plague them every step of the way. Their plight seems to be taking them to nowhere.

However, that is where the similarities end. *The Man without a Country* is historical fiction. Mr. Nolan was a man convicted of treason. Our story is true and our 'little people' can be tried for nothing. They were beautiful, scar-free innocence until the perpetrators decided to make their moves.

Some people call these little wards of the courts *kids*. We, too, will call them kids later in the story, but for now we want you to know they are 'little people.' They missed that happiness train to childhood. Their innocence was betrayed. Their trust was violated. Their safety was forfeited.

Many woke up to the wickedness, sickness, and horrible maladies in the cradle. So, yes, they are wise and educated and well-versed in ways that you and I may never comprehend.

We are going to minutely touch on the atrocities here. Later we will also share the grim public opinion the 'little people' must face as they continue to strive to be 'normal.'

State workers are rarely surprised by the abuses 'little people' suffer because rape, physical beatings or torture, neglect, and starvation are not uncommon. As we share our adopted kids' stories with you, you will know they suffered some or all of the above violations.

When the 'little people' are placed in foster homes or are adopted, the baggage goes with them. Some have violent episodes, including screaming, acting out, cursing, and even personal attack.

If a situation becomes so volatile that injury is a risk, foster parents must restrain the child in a lock-down position. They do this by rocking the child onto his back and pulling his knees up by his head. The position is uncomfortable, but not painful. After the great release of anger, hurt, and humiliation, exhaustion and calm settle in. Conversation, reason, and corrective strategies may begin.

We are going to share some of these incidences with you; however, we won't linger on these topics long because our focus is the amazing resiliency and renewal many of these 'little people' discover as they grow older. Once they know, understand, and utilize the power of *CHOICE*, they are on the way to recovery.

We believe strongly that the revelation of choice is a life-changing experience for these young men and women. So we have set up a non-profit *Fund of Choice Organization* to financially assist deserving young adults who were raised in foster or adoptive homes. Designated proceeds from the purchase of this book help fund the organization.

Our final wish is to secure more homes for the foster children in America. There were 17,438 foreign adoptions in the United States in 2008 according to *USA Today*. Foreign adoption is noble. However, those who adopt at home are not only saving a child, but they are also helping make our nation stronger!

Seventeen thousand five hundred adoptions in this country would only leave a little over 109,000 homes needed!

It's All About
CHOICE

Chapter 1

The Crazy Folks Down the Road

Her eyes were red and bloodshot; her shrill screams, profanities and vulgarities were unceasing; and her fight gained momentum as the adrenaline surged into her system.

Kicking and clawing were her tools for revenge—revenge upon her biological roots, the system, relatives or anyone else who knew about the abuse and did nothing, her foster parents, and most of the entire world!

It didn't matter at this point. Everyone was a foe. No one could be trusted. Violation after violation had taken its toll.

Our only hope to subdue her with dignity was to apply the hold. I slipped my arm under her knees and pulled them up by her head. I clamped into a vice stronghold.

"It's okay," we whispered. "Scream it out. Yell your obscenities. You have every right. We have you tight in our arms. When you tire, when you exhaust yourself, we will talk. So scream, baby, scream. Get it out. Get it all out!"

Part of this message was audible, coaxing our new foster child to max-out and reach her melting point. Part of the message was in my head as I concentrated on holding her for her own protection. Time seemed forever as the tirade continued. My wife's support sustained me. Her soothing words to our foster child were also therapeutic for me, helping me to continue. Finally, our child began to pant for breath between the screams.

"Good," I thought. "She is beginning to tire."

Sometimes the pants were a sure sign the episode would end soon. Sometimes the pants were like a woman's false labor pains. They only announced the coming of the real thing. We knew if we survived the second onslaught, we would be home free. We continued. We held fast until our child's body became limp and the soft sobbing and hiccupping were for real.

Then we talked. First we talked in the hold, continuing to protect and sooth and support. We slowly loosened our grip as her first inaudible venting became language we could understand. Now the real work began.

This camera shot moment in our lives as foster parents describes an abused child's release of pent-up fear, rage, humiliation, and loss of self. It is the essence of someone trying to find their soul again. This child's abuse had many faces. All were perverted. All were sick. But the one that yielded the greatest punch, wrestling her identity from her, was sexual abuse.

In his book, *A Child Called It*, Dave Pelzer tells about the abuse he endured for almost a decade. He describes how his mother beat him; fed him household ammonia and Clorox, rubbed his face in fecal matter, gassed him with a mixture of household products, starved him, burned him, and even stabbed him just inside his rib cage.

This is not an exhaustive list of the abuses Mr. Pelzer suffered. He describes these abuses and many more in minute detail as only a person 'who has been there' could.

Mr. Pelzer's book has been on the New York Best Seller list for six years and many city public libraries have a double-digit waiting list for borrowing it.

In his book, Mr. Pelzer said he thought he was alone through all those years of abuse. However, after he was finally 'saved' and began to grow older, he said he realized that he was not alone. At the time he wrote his book, over 3 million children were being abused in the United States. That is approximately one in five children.

As we think about the many years that Mr. Pelzer was abused, it is difficult to imagine how his father, brothers, and relatives could bury themselves so deep in denial that they could allow the abuse to continue. And this portrait of denial makes one ask a profound question: How could neighbors, clergy, doctors, teachers and others read the innuendoes and pinpoint signs of the abuse and still do nothing?

Then the quest for answers becomes even more mind boggling when we multiply the family, neighbors, clergy, doctors, and teachers times 3 million children! That number becomes astronomical.

Mr. Pelzer's story describes other abused children's plights as well. He writes that the abuse finally began to take its toll on him. He slowly slipped into nothingness, feeling he was a no one even before his mother actually called him an *"it."*

He described how abuse perpetuated itself in and

outside the home. After enduring beatings at home, he became the bully's punching bag at school. Many folks who didn't know or understand looked down upon him.

These phenomena are common among all abused children. It is the very nature of abuse. Children are used, violated, manipulated, and badgered into oblivion. This is the perpetrator's power!

Children are not removed from their biological homes until abuse, neglect, or other gross violations have been documented. The foster child's outbursts, tantrums, and acting-out are, in part, efforts to reestablish their being—to regain a sense of self.

According to the California social services, Dave Pelzer's case is considered *one of the most severe child abuse cases in California history.*

However, without taking away from the atrocities Mr. Pelzer suffered and his amazing ability to survive and later thrive, I wonder how one can measure abuse.

Is one type of abuse really more horrid than another?

Is it worse to wake up each morning with no food in your stomach or to wake up seeing your father's private anatomy staring you in the face?

The spirit is violated by any form of abuse and all

abuse is life threatening in some way - mentally, emotionally, or physically. Following different pathways, the abuse may even cause multiple deaths, one type of death after the other.

These are important questions to ask because when we believe Mr. Pelzer's story is unique, when we forget that he did not suffer alone, we tend to minimize the problem. Mr. Pelzer is okay now, we say. We think our job is finished. We think the problem has been remedied.

So we want to speak in reality here. We want to awaken those with the tools to make a difference - those who have big hearts for the young American who is lost and bewildered.

What are sketches of foster parents? Who can do the job? The social service agencies advertise that foster and adoptive parents need not be wealthy.

It is true; a family does not need to be wealthy. However, it is our experience that a little money is definitely a needed commodity. If I were to describe potential foster parents in one word, it would be mavericks.

All early Americans were considered mavericks. They were unafraid and venturesome. They were known as nonconformists. They didn't worry about the neighbors. They did their own things, moved on when they felt the calling, and dealt with anyone who attempted to get in their way—sometimes gently, sometimes more forcefully.

They blazed trails. The unknown was a challenge to them rather than an obstacle. Since almost everything was unknown in the new world, the very fact they were standing on American soil made them trail blazers.

My and my wife's stories demonstrate that anyone can be a trail blazer. We Americans are more alike than different. I hope you identify.

I have been called a maverick on more than one occasion. Sometimes I feel for my poor wife. I am highly energetic and work on multiple projects simultaneously.

It is nothing to have half-dozen projects in the making and still start a new one. Others have told me, "Wow, when you work, you work hard. When you play, you play hard."

Part of who we are is innate. Part of who we are is learned. I guess my high energy was always there. At least I was told I nearly jumped out of the cradle in the delivery room. I guess I squealed and squawked and rolled over at least once in the nursery. I have been doing that ever since.

Everyone has trials and hardships as they grow up.

Growing up is rarely easy for anyone. I was no exception. But these times make a person who they are. When it all boils down to the nitty-gritty our personal choices are what really matter.

School was not easy for me. I had everyone scratching their heads until they gave a name to my problem. I am dyslexic. This means that I see the written word and numbers backwards much of the time. So starting in first grade, the kids nicknamed me Dumbert.

My mother unknowingly compounded this problem. She was young and thought that dressing her kids the BEST was a sign of her love. So I went to school in dress clothes when the other kids wore jeans. This gave the kids more ammunition. They added 'Doctor' to my nickname list.

Here I was. I thought c-a-t was spelled t-a-c and I wore white jeans, a dress shirt, and white athletic sweater on Jr. High game days. No wonder the kids called me 'Dumbert' and 'Doctor.'

I joke about this now, but it was very traumatic at the time. I carried the name Dumbert all through grade school. I thought I was doomed to be Dumbert the rest of my life, but an angel came to my rescue in 7th grade.

Our football coach, Johnny Craig, came out on the

field. He gave me a look that I didn't understand and said, "Delbert, come over here and stand."

He stretched out his arm to show me where to go. Then he walked over to the other boys on the team. "Make a circle around Delbert," he said.

The boys circled around me. Then Coach continued, "If you can hold Delbert in this circle, you may continue to call him Dumbert. However, if you cannot hold him in the circle, if you allow him to bust through the line, you must rename him *Harvey Wallbanger!*"

My name changed that day. My relationship with my peers changed. In fact, the direction of my entire life changed because a coach named Johnnie Craig cared to make a difference!

Life depends on how you look at it. I could still cry about my unhappy first years in school or I can choose to see what these experiences did for me. They helped me become independent and stand alone rather than join the crowd. They helped me have empathy for others, fighting for the underdog when bullies taunted and teased. And they helped me feel others' pain.

These are the things that made me say, "You know what? I think I can love foster children as my own. I think I can endure so I am not a turning, twisting twig in their lives, but a solid rock instead."

Christie's story is different from mine. She was placed in a foster home at age five. It was a loving home, but the family chose only to do foster care. She was a beautiful little girl, with big impressive eyes, a sweet face, and soft natural curls. So she was very adoptable and was placed in a permanent home at age seven.

Christie's adoptive family was a loving family as well. Her adoptive father was a farmer and the family was deeply rooted in the community and church.

Christie jokes about being in church every Sunday morning, every Sunday evening, Wednesday night prayer service and any other time the doors were open. Then she laughs and adds, "And we were there many times when the doors weren't open!"

Some people who experience early trauma and have lived in foster care tend to make their past the topic of conversation. However, others shy away from sharing any information at all. Christie is like that. I am probably one of the few people in the world who knows most of her story. I say most of her story because I'm sure that she has withheld some information even from me.

I remember many positive things people said to me when I was a child. People told me that I had a big heart. They told me that I was a hard worker; they told me that I was trustworthy. But when I ask Christie what good things people said about her as a child, she doesn't remember anything.

I know someone must have told her she was beautiful because she is; I know someone must have told her she has an uncanny ability to listen without interjecting opinion, because she does. Since I know her virtues, it is difficult for me to imagine that she did not receive some positive feedback.

This has, at times, been perplexing to me. I have wondered: "When a child protects herself by blocking the constant barrage of violations against her, does she also block positive affirmations in the process? Must all information go because a child must deny most of it?"

However, I don't analyze the question long because Christie quickly provides a solid explanation for her refusal to dwell in the past: "The past is the past," she explains, "and re-churning the facts encourages regression. I have made the choice to move forward." So she *chooses* to share her information only when it will directly benefit another.

Christie has done that. She has utilized her past for the future. She made the choice to adopt seven children who were given up for lost. She washed,

cooked, scrubbed, nursed, taught, confronted, con-
soled, nurtured, and—yes—endured to give others the
same hope she received herself.

It is amazing how often that little six-letter word—
choice—has emerged within these few short pages.
We have talked about the violator's choice to perpe-
trate, the people's choice to refuse to become
involved, and the community's choice to emulate the
perpetrator's abusive role through cutting remarks
and condescending attitudes.

However, for every bad choice, there is a good
choice. The choice of an awesome coach who cares
enough to help change a child's life, the story of a
survivor-child who chooses to use his story for positive change for others, and our choices, like thousands of other foster parents in America, to help give
America's throw-away "it" children a new perspective,
a new hope, and a new identity.

All these choices are important. They are important in identifying society's problems and promoting
workable solutions. However, the most phenomenal,
most far-reaching choice of all is the choice of the
abused baby, child, or young adult to survive, make a
new history, and become a positive impact upon this
world.

As David Pelzer wrote in his book:

> *"My dark past is behind me now. As bad as it was, I knew even back then, in the final analysis, my way of life would be up to me. I made a promise to myself that if I came out of my situation alive; I had to make something of myself. I would be the best person that I could be."*

If Dave Pelzer emerged victorious from his horrible, abusive, violent past, anyone can win through choice and determination. Mr. Pelzer's victory over his plight makes most of us look like wimps in comparison.

However, we personally know some of those kids who were "its" for a time - kids who have survived and have now become the CEOs of their own lives.

This is their story.

Chapter 2

The Reason for the Season

Vincent

Sim and the other guys from school were congregated on the corner of Main Street. When they saw my pickup, they started waving. I stopped, knowing that I really shouldn't.

"Hey, man," the guys said. They were all talking at once, except for Sim. He was standing to the side with a smart-alecky grin on his face. So I had to listen with both ears to catch the gist of the plan.

"Vince, want to chip in on the bet?"

"Is there some kind of bet going on here? I'm broke to the bone. What's going on?" I asked.

"Sim said he's going to streak down Main Street. We've got a bet going that he's too chicken to do it. Are you in on the bet or not?"

"Tell you what. As I said, I'm broke to the bone. I just got off work and I'm delivering the close-out money to the Dairy Queen (DQ) manager. I'll do a quick deliver and then I'll be right back."

"Well, we can't wait for the answer. What is it? Are you in or out?"

"I'm in, not with money, but I'll be 'in' with the body."

"You're what?" they questioned in anticipation.

"If Sim streaks, I streak! End of conversation. I'll be back in a split second."

"I just made points and I really didn't have to do anything to get them," I thought as I drove toward the DQ manager's home. "Sim isn't going to streak - not in a million years. This is one humongous joke!"

To my surprise, Sim was nearly down to the skin when I returned. All the guys were cheering and teasing, telling me to "put up or shut up."

My gut began to twist and churn. I hadn't been in trouble for awhile now. Maybe this would go without a hitch. Maybe no one would really notice. My word was my word. I had to do it.

Sim and I got down to the bare and then decided

to wear our athletic jackets and our tennis shoes on our trek down Main Street. With the guys cheering and laughing, we took off.

Well, what I had hoped would remain unnoticed became noticed.

My parents asked me about the incident and I *kind* of regressed to old ways.

I told them the streaking was for real. I just didn't tell them that I was one of the streakers! This was not a good idea. When Mom and Dad found out, I was grounded for six months. I learned very vividly that day that withholding pertinent information constitutes a grand, full-blown lie! Mom and Dad punished more severely for lies than anything else we might do.

As part of my punishment, I had to continue to pay for the pickup that I had just bought, but I couldn't drive it. I was allowed to go to school, work, athletic practice, and school games. These were all solid commitments for my education, to the team, and for a successful future.

All social engagements were cancelled, barred, nil. At first, I thought this was outlandish punishment. Six months' pay for a three-minute run down Main Street in my 'birthday suit' seemed really harsh to me.

However, today, I see it as a plausible, well

thought-out plan. This punishment forced me to concentrate on my studies and my commitment to others.

I probably accomplished more in that six-month period than I usually did within a year's time.

The real truth is that the two people who were responsible for giving me birth taught me how to sabotage myself. My parents, those people who adopted me into their family, helped teach me how to become a responsible, caring, and successful individual.

My name is Vincent and I was eleven years old when I moved into Mom and Dad's home. I suffered many of the abuses mentioned in this book. So I will not go into detail about the scourges in my life. I will say that I learned very young in life to protect ME.

I guess that is one of the reasons that I was on the "ship to nowhere" for many years. I bounced from one foster home to another, reaching a total of nine foster homes in a short time. The system had given up on me. I was headed for a Level 5 group home if Mom and Dad's home didn't work out for me.

I wasn't concerned about tomorrow. I was all about surviving today. I was adept at manipulation, bribery, reading and playing one person against another. All maneuvers were aimed for my personal satisfaction.

No one was going to keep me, love me, or save me. I needed to get to them first so I wouldn't be hurt again!

I craved chaos. So I churned chaos everywhere I went. I played the foster father against the foster mother. Then I reversed my strategy and played the foster mother against the foster father.

I know this sounds like a lot of gibberish, but it really is great for dysfunctional maneuvering. It works to play one against the other and then reverse the tactic. In fact, the reversal is necessary to keep the couple in turmoil and, yet, keep them clueless for as long as possible about what is really taking place.

If there were siblings, I could really get it going. I could have siblings fighting with parents and with each other. And, of course, I was always in the middle somewhere.

I always knew that I was in a home for a *reason*. The couple needed money, the couple wanted to replace a lost child, the couple wanted a second chance to raise a caretaker, or a million other reasons. That made me a solid 'it'. I was a *reason*, not a person.

Sometimes this made me feel important in a sick sort of way, but most of the time it made me feel used.

Now I was with Mom and Dad. It was another

home, another chance to destroy the myth that foster children can find permanent homes and live happily ever after.

I lied. I acted out. I hid things. One of my favorite hiding items was Mom's nebulizer that she used to relieve her asthma. If I hid it, it caused the stress and chaos that I was craving.

The system had told Mom and Dad that I was not adoptable. They classed me an incorrigible—incurable, hopeless. I didn't hear this message and don't know that I was actually aware that I was trying to prove them right. But now I see that I was bent on this objective.

I fought with the kids at school. I didn't get along with the teachers. I tried to cause problems everywhere I went. I began to projectile vomit at some point. I'm not sure if this was a ploy to get what I wanted or if it was frustration because Dad said "You may not know it yet, but you have just met up with the most stubborn man this side of heaven."

Mom and Dad didn't baby me; Dad put me in his hold many times when I acted out. It wasn't painful to lay there with my knees beside my head. It was just a bit uncomfortable.

However, the secure hold, the human touch, was giving me a message: "I wouldn't be holding you

here, if I didn't care. I would say 'Be gone with you!'
and go on with my life. I am here because I choose to
be here."

In retrospect, I can see the hold was supportive
rather than a punishment to me. Also, Dad talked a
lot about personal choice and responsibility. He told
us we had the power to change the direction of our
lives. He said our future was in our own hands.
These things made the difference in my life. In fact, I
believe they ignited the beginning - the beginning of
my new self. Dad always said, "Vincent, it is your
choice how you respond to others."

I watched and listened. I began to see that I
thought differently than my peers did. As I analyzed
my thought processes, an amazing thing happened. I
realized that I was no dummy.

To do what I had been doing all my life - the
maneuvering and manipulating - took brains! "What
if," I thought, "I used my intellect for something positive like Mom and Dad preach for me to do?"

My life began to take a different direction. Some
people, including a couple of teachers, couldn't
change with me. They were still stuck with the old
Vincent. I guess they were just human; and since
change is a gradual thing with forward and backward
movements, they may have had trouble keeping up

until permanent change was an undeniable, observable fact.

One day I told Dad that I didn't realize he was counseling me all those years until it was too late. I became a good kid before I knew it.

This is part of my story. There will be more about me later, telling how I continued to grow and became the person that I am today.

Mitch

Dear Addiction,

I thought you were my boy. We've been through some good times.

Whenever I was down, you were there to pick me up. Whenever I was up, you were there to take me higher. Remember all those times I got locked up? You were always there when I got out, kicking it with me. All I'm saying is you've always had my back and that's some real deal. But we ain't kicked it since my last arrest. Sometimes I miss you.

But the other week, I was holding my son in my arms as he fell asleep. He is seven months old now. Can you believe that?

And I had something come over me as I was holding him in my arms with tears streaming down my face. He had his arms folded across his chest just like me when I sleep.

At that moment of clarity, I realized that you ain't been there for me at all. You have only been there when I wanted an easy way out and wanted to screw up my life. I realized that you are turning me into the very same thing as my birth parents.

I don't know how I could ever let you help me screw up so badly. You ain't my boy and darn sure ain't my friend. You have only been there at my time of weakness.

So from this day forward, I am going to part ways with you and put my life back together. It's not just about me anymore. I have found someone to take your place. This 'little guy' can take me to much higher levels of happiness than you ever have or ever could.

So peace, goodbye, and down with you!
Mitch

Dear Dad,

I'm going to start our conversation with – WOW! I've never met a person in the world with a heart bigger than yours. I first showed up at your doorstep and thought, "Great, the 27th foster home. I wonder how long this one is going to last."

As time went on, things went pretty well. Day after day passed and I grew fond of my surroundings. I thought *it would be pretty nice to stay awhile.*

Then you and Mom sat me down. An instant of fear and rejection came over me. I was thinking,"Great! Now I'm going on to the next place!" But, to my surprise, you asked me a question: "What do you think about us adopting you?"

I was dumbfounded. I was at a loss for words. Then you added, "Before you give us your answer, you need to know something. It's not always going to be a bed of roses."

All I could think was, "How could you treat me any different than you have in the past?"

I finally found out what 'roses' meant. And on top of that, you adopted my brothers – Cody and Machi. That's some real deal!

You saw something in me that no one else ever has and you gave me the time of day that no one else would.

But what is most amazing to me to this day is how a man can bring a child into his home, among others who are not his, and love them as his own.

You have given me so many chances and, in return, I have done nothing but disappoint you and kick you in the rear. But never once have you given up on me – despite that I felt that way at times.

You have saved my life in many ways that I can't explain. And for that I can never say that I love you enough or thank you enough.

You are, hands down, the biggest man I know and, by far, the best role model I have ever had.
Mitch

Dear Mom,

I am not sure where to start and where to end. You are such a great person. I could never put into words what you mean to me. You have always been by my side through thick and thin as if I were your own blood. You never thought twice.

I know it was tough to be unable to have kids of your own, but, to be truthful, I'm glad because I would never have had this chance to make it this far.

I owe you more than I could ever repay because, in many ways, you are playing one of the biggest parts in my sobriety and you don't even know it.

I remember the day Tina came home and said she was pregnant. I felt so alone and in disbelief. You were the first person I called. I told you that I had thought strongly about abortion. I had decided abortion was the answer because I was in no position to support a child in this world.

I felt your heart sink as much as mine. I knew this would be your first grandchild.

Instead of the two-hour lecture that I expected, you

simply said, "No."

You said the baby would be born.

I said, "Fine. I'll put it up for adoption at birth to make sure it has a life that I can't provide."

Again, you simply said, "Okay." Then you continued, "If you do that, Dad and I will adopt him."

You placed me in a situation that I now respect and understand. My son gave me the clarity and reason for cleaning up my life.

I love you more than you will ever know and again thank you for everything.

Mitch

I'm Mitch and these letters were written in drug rehabilitation. These letters were a promise for positive changes in my life.

I don't ever remember being a child. I remember worrying about feeding my younger siblings from the beginning. I say "beginning" because I can't remember anything before that.

I fetched alcohol for my father upon demand, knowing that the drunker he became the harder he beat me and the others. To make the beating feel a little bit worse, he always poured rice on the floor. Then making us kneel on rice, he took the whip to us.

Sometimes he locked us in closets and held us in

the dark. He did anything that might heighten his drunken stupors. The Catholic Church was nearby and I remember that I could always depend upon them for food for my siblings. So I could spend my time working on other survival techniques.

Mom wasn't there. Oh, she came home for short periods of time, but then would leave again to shack up with another man somewhere. She, too, was wrapped up in the drug and alcohol scene.

Once when I was very small, my heart craved for her to come home. We needed her for some reason which my mind does not want to remember.

What I do remember is searching for her. I walked across town and found the house where she was staying. I knocked on the door. A man, brusque and unkempt, answered the door. He asked me what I was doing there.

I remember looking up into those bloodshot eyes and begging with all my heart, "Can my mommy come home now?"

Then I went home alone.

When our family was rescued, we kids were separated. Years later Cody, Machi, and I were reunited at our permanent adopted home.

The going was really rough at times for Mom and Dad. After I attended a beer party in the country, some of the crowd brought me home in a blackout condition.

When Dad saw me, he knew. He yelled, "Don't take him out of the car. Take him straight to the hospital!"

That yell and demand saved my life because I was suffering from alcohol poisoning. The doctor said I would have been dead in short order if I had not received treatment.

Dad and Mom are realists. They don't bury their heads in denial. When the other kids' dads were hiding their alcohol and drug usage, my Dad was calling the police on me.

One time Mom and Dad were going out of town. Dad warned that he would turn us in if we had a beer party in his home.

When they returned, we were having a beer party. He called the police. I received a citation for minor in possession and so did the other kids who attended. The other parents were not happy and Dad received scorn from them for his actions. Dad took it in stride. He always said, "Excuses for wrong-doing never makes anyone a better person!" He meant it and he enforced it when he was in authority.

My letter to Dad said that he believed in me and saw things in me that no one else ever did. He has always told me I have a special gift. He told me so often that I began to believe him. I know that I can build almost anything; I love to mechanic and seem to see things that others don't on repair and maintenance.

These talents have benefited my family financially and have helped me believe in myself and my ability to provide.

Machi

I am Machi. I am Cody and Mitch's little brother. I too had to kneel on rice and take beatings when father was drinking. I too was left at home with nothing to eat while Mom visited with the community men.

Mitch did well for the rest of us kids. I don't remember ever being hungry because Mitch always brought us food from the church. I was the baby and I was treated like that.

Some things were pretty wrong with me though, because I was hospitalized for a time. I really don't understand what was wrong with me. I just know it was a hospital for the mentally ill and that I was a pretty tiny guy at the time.

When I came to live with Mom and Dad, my life

changed too - like my brothers' did. Mom and Dad
talked differently than anyone else ever had. They
told me that I was a good kid. I hadn't heard that too
many times in my life. Sometimes they laughed at me
and forgot to punish me. They said, "Your cute smile
just wins us over."

One time Mom left some powdered sugar donuts
on the counter top. I took half the sack downstairs to
my room. I sat on the edge of my bed and gobbled all
but a donut or two. Then I plopped back on my bed
and fell asleep.

What I didn't know was that Mom found the
empty donut bag on the counter. She started making
the rounds.

She went from bedroom to bedroom looking for
signs of the culprit. When I woke up she said,
"Machi, why did you eat all the donuts?"

Sitting there with white powder all over my
mouth and two donuts laying beside me on the bed, I
said, "Who me? I didn't eat any donuts!"

Mom didn't make a federal case out of it. She
laughed and then talked to me. I guess she thought it
was a kid thing rather than a big theft deal. She let
me know that I could eat anything in the house, but
half a sack of donuts was kind of out-of-the-ordinary.
This helped me learn that kids do kids' things some-

times, and that I was no different.

I cried often when I realized my brothers were doing drugs. I not only worried for them, but I didn't want to follow in their footsteps. I wanted to become strong and independent immediately. It didn't happen.

I secretly started smoking while I was still in high school and after I graduated, I fell into many of the pitfalls my brothers had. To my chagrin, I also spent time in jail after I left home and enrolled in a trade school.

I think my parents were especially devastated because they had such great hopes for me.

I know it seems strange to someone reading this that I cried because I didn't want to do what my brothers were doing. Yet, I ended up following in their footsteps. I think I am an example that the first two years of our lives are extremely important.

Even though I really don't remember a lot, my first years seemed to affect everything I did. I, too, had to get to the age of accountability to understand that the choices for me are now my choices and my destiny is in my own hands.

The Others

There are others who are not sharing yet. There were seven of us foster kids adopted into Mom and Dad's home and over fifty other children who passed through. Many of the fifty were reunited with their biological families, some were adopted by relatives, and some were emancipated, making a choice to live on their own.

Our three remaining siblings have chosen to stay out of the lime-light for various reasons. They may not be ready to share or they may not have reached the moment of clarity for change.

Only they know the real reason. Everyone travels at his or her own pace and some never realize a new self. They stay victims their entire lives.

We hope and pray that our siblings do understand their personal power of choice and choose to stay silent because that is their style.

Rashona

Rashona is the little light that helped tie us all together. Mom and Dad adopted her free of baggage and past. She came to us directly from the hospital. We were all delighted. It was as if Mom was expecting and we all witnessed the birthing process.

Rashona is beautiful. She boasts a mixed heritage which is symbolic of us and our various backgrounds. Rashona is African American, American Indian, and Caucasian.

All seven of us and Tanner, the one and only biological child in Mom and Dad's family, included Rashona in one of our senior pictures. The pictures are all lined up on the family room wall.

We joke that when we went to-get-her we came *together*.

Chapter 3

Odd Man Out

Tanner

I wasn't on that ship to nowhere, bouncing from foster home to foster home. I had two homes with parents who loved me and wanted me. My biological parents were divorced when I was a baby. Each remarried and worked at being civil, and even congenial for my sake, but periodic spats did occur.

I chose to live in Dad's home at about age ten. Even though I don't know about the 'it' thing and I don't know about living in twenty-seven different homes, I do know what it is like being the *odd man out.*

When I was at Mom's, I had three half-sisters. When I was at Dad's, I had brothers and sisters coming and going on a continual basis. I was Dad's only biological child, but I had to share him with a townload of kids.

Dad was especially tough on me. My siblings have attested to the fact that Dad was a stickler on many things, but with me it was even tougher.

The others always played the biological favorite thing with him and he either believed it or he just wanted me to measure up as the example.

I think there is something that he may have overlooked. Even though I didn't carry the same baggage as the foster kids did, I had some of my own. Also, some of the foster kids' baggage was lethal and when they came into our home, they brought their poison with them.

What the average person doesn't realize is over 50 half-grown kids came through our home. They weren't just out of the cradle; most were cunning con artists wise beyond their years. Most of them were masterfully adept at getting to you before you could get to them!

I'm not trying to gain sympathy or wallow in a great big pity party. I'm just trying to be truthful. As Dad said many times, "Don't expect a bed of roses."

No one has them all their life and we were no exception.

The truth is that I love all my adopted siblings as well as my half- sisters. Cody and I are about the same age. We ran track together in high school. We were very closely matched and would come in one behind the other. We would plan out the run and then congratulate each other as we finished one-two over the line. That was great!

We shared the same bedroom at home and were like real blood-brothers. I was closer to him than most of the others.

I was an underachiever in school. I was diagnosed with Attention Deficit Disorder and I didn't exert much effort. I would hang loose and date the girls rather than apply myself.

I suffered from some of the same self-esteem problems that my siblings did and I started on a downward slide after high school. I went to a neighboring city and got into some pretty heavy stuff. I was doing what I knew I shouldn't be doing and I was uneasy about it. Finally, I woke up one morning and said, "I can go on this way or I can save myself before it is too late."

I got up out of bed and called Dad. "I'm ready," I said. "I am ready to go to school and make something of myself."

"Good," he said. "I have been waiting to hear those words. I am glad you have made that choice. When do you want to enroll? I will do everything I can to help you get started."

That is one thing about Dad. He refuses to be an enabler. So as long as we were on a binge, he let us binge without his help. When we made the right choice – the choice for good citizenry and personal success, he was on board without a lecture and without an apology from us.

He always made money accessible to us, but never gave it directly. We had a dog kennel and the dogs provided income for all of us at one time. We also had cattle on our grandfather's farm which was a potential income source, depending upon how much we wanted to put into it.

When we became too big or too good to do the chores, we also forfeited the income. The amazing thing about that is even though we knew it was our choice, most of us blew it for awhile anyway.

I think each of us lost everything at one time as we were venturing out on our own. We lost our vehicles. We lost our cattle money. We lost our kennel money.

Dad believes in accountability and personal responsibility. When we were *'out to lunch,'* he didn't carry the load.

We could have kept our vehicles if we could have made the payments, if we could buy insurance, and if we could purchase the tags. But the fact was that when we were on a binge, we didn't work. If we didn't work, we lost our interest in our money-making projects. That was just a fact of life and we knew it.

Chapter 4

The Heart of It

"Mamma, Mamma," Rashona cried. "He ate it. He really ate it!"

"Who ate? . . . Ate what?" Christie questioned.

"Machi did it. He ate my hot dog!"

"He ate your hot dog? We don't have any hot dogs. Where did you get a hot dog?"

Rashona's ebony cheeks were flushed. Her loose black ringlets bounced up and down as she swished herself into place for an out-and-out explanation.

"Mom," she said in exasperated respect, "I made the hot dogs out of my play dough! Machi came into the room, grabbed it, and took a bite. It was a big bite, Mom. It wasn't a little bite. Now it's half gone!"

"Rashona, Machi didn't really eat play dough," Christie explained.

"Yes, he did. Yes, he did. Oh, yes, he did. I know, Mom. Machi really ate it. He even said, "MMMmmmmm –good!"

Machi came into the room wearing his usual spunky, half-grin. He was the baby of the family for a long time before Rashona arrived. Everyone's drawn to him because of his quiet, sweet nature. His style of teasing is always a reflection of his good-hearted spirit.

"Rashona," he said. "MMMMMmmm you sure do make good hot dogs. Thanks for that one, little moment of bliss."

"Machi, I'm going to get you."

Rashona darted after Machi as he skipped out of the room laughing and squealing. A moment later, Rashona peeked around the kitchen door. "Mom," she said with a grin. "Machi is still my favorite brother."

"Even - - if - - he - - ate - - my - - hotdog - - - - -!" Her voice echoed as she ran after Machi again.

It was neat to watch Rashona with the other kids. They gave her lots of love and attention. Sometimes the attention was teasing. Sometimes it was a quiet smile. When she was a baby, they would even rock and cuddle her.

I must confess Christie and I used the protective attitude the other kids had for Rashona to our advantage sometimes.

We didn't allow swearing in our home. If we heard the kids using foul language, they had to pay-up. Then we spent the money on Rashona. We always told them,"Rashona won't benefit from your raunchy language, but she certainly will benefit from your remorse. Dig into your pockets and put a coin in the jar for every bad word you uttered." No one ever argued the point. They dug in and paid up.

In many ways our family is like any other family. We have hopes and dreams. We work, go to school, play, and vacation. However, we are also very different. We have issues as all families have issues, but some of our issues are unique.

Not every family has several children who were groomed in infancy to develop survival techniques, and not every family has a son who missed every family vacation because he was *"too bad"* to go.

Three of our children are biological brothers. They were adopted into a home at one point in their short histories. Mitch was one of the brothers who lived in that home, but he was not adoptable according to the system and the adoptive parents.

So the family allowed Mitch to live in their home, but they would not adopt him. When the family went on vacation, Mitch's brothers went, but he was placed in respite care. He knew he was "too bad" to go with them.

One year after Mitch came to live with us, we decided to go to South Padre Island for vacation. Christie and I decided to surprise the kids and tell them at supper.

We passed the food and after everyone had filled their plates, we began. "Hang on to your hats, guys and gals; we have extra special news for you. We are going to go on a grand vacation!"

I looked around the table. Everyone was sitting perfectly still, looking at us in wide-eyed anticipation. Everyone except Mitch, that is. He concentrated on looking at his plate as he continued eating, slowly and methodically pushing his spoon into the food as a crane shovel digs into the dirt. His expression was blank. His emotion was locked inside.

"Where are we going?" everyone asked at once.

"We're going to South Padre Island!" we proudly announced.

The room buzzed with excitement as seven kids began chattering, questioning and giggling about adventure and fun on South Padre Island.

> *"Where is South Padre Island? Is it in this country?"*

> *"Yes, corn-ball; it is in Texas."*

> *"What will we do there – deep sea dive, chase elephants, climb the trees with the monkeys?"*

> *"South Padre Island? What is a South Padre Island?"*

> *"An island is surrounded by water, silly, don't you know that?"*

> *"Oh, duh, then we'll swim there, right?"*

Mitch had stopped digging at his food and was sitting motionless and quiet. "Aren't you happy about the vacation, Mitch?" I asked.

"Where will *I* stay," he answered as he continued to stare at his food.

"Well, for starters, you may stay in a few Holiday Inns.

You may sleep in a cabin at some point. Or how about staying in the tent one night?" I continued to list the overnight possibilities.

"What does that mean?" he mumbled without looking up. "I just want to know who I'm staying with."

"You're going with us, Mitch. You're going. Do you understand me? There is no respite care for you this time. You are part of the family."

"You mean I'm going with you? I'm really going on vacation?" He looked up at me as his eyes began to fill with tears. "I've never gone on vacation with the family before. I was too bad to go with them."

"Well, you are not too bad to go with us," I said. "You'd better get up and get busy, boy, because you have some packing and planning to do. You're going and you're going to have a ball!"

Mitch sat in disbelief for a moment longer. Then he timidly joined the others as they made wonderful, extravagant predictions about their time on the island.

The family who wouldn't adopt Mitch had adopted Machi. Machi was a toddler at the time.

We were told that Machi had such a "lively spirit" the family felt they needed to medicate him to calm him down.

However, he ultimately became so "calm" that he had to be hospitalized to bring him out of it. Later this family returned all the boys to the system.

Christie and I had a hard time understanding why someone would medicate Machi. In our presence he was an adorable, quiet child with a winning smile. We never saw the lively spirit that needed tamed. We know children react differently with different people so we tried not to judge.

However, we do know this is part of the continual plight for America's foster child. Sometimes they do find a place to call home, but too many times it isn't for long.

The children are moved again for whatever reason, and they don't understand what happened. Many of them believe that it was their fault. They believe they are contaminated, used goods that will continue to go from house to house forever.

One time in a family gab session, Cody put it this way:

"Foster children are like used cars. Some of them are okay, but most are lemons and then discarded!"

The system helps cement this concept into place when they advertise the children like used cars, business supplies, or other commodity over the internet or on newscasts.

If a child is advertised and immediately adopted, there may be no harm. However, when an abused, insecure, violated child is advertised for 'give-away' and no one answers the call, the self-hatred and stigma surrounding them thickens, hardens, and becomes immovable! Even though our story is about choice, not about blame, we must say *'shame on them'* for this practice.

For a system supposedly filled with child care credentials, it is hard to imagine how this practice escaped their attention and flourishes to further degrade many of the foster children in this country. In our opinion, if one little soul is marred or injured due to this practice, the whole idea is worthless - defunct!

However, the prejudice and the ignorance of many people and community systems may make this practice pale in comparison.

The next chapter of this book will share crises situations. It will help explain the ongoing plight of the foster child even after they are adopted.

It is the hardest to stomach. It is the hardest to tell. It is the most difficult for the child to surmount!

Chapter 5

The Crescendos

"The one thing about foster children," he said, "is they are like the plague. You just can't get rid of them!"

When the social service case worker reported the principal's remark, we didn't realize that she was also summing up the feelings of many others in our community. We were still under the illusion that everyone respects those who try to make a difference.

There were two families in town that had foster children so the school was getting a double dose of reality. Foster children may have magnified issues, depending upon the level of abuse they endured.

Society must pick up the tab for the perpetrators' sicknesses and schools must be front runners in the rehabilitation process.

This principal's remark clearly stated his stance. He was not willing to work with us and he was not interested in providing a stepping stone for the children's renewal and success.

Through the years, I found myself darkening the school's doorstep on many occasions.

The administration changed several times and some were easier to work with than others.

On one occasion, a young man touched one of our foster daughters inappropriately in the school halls. She complained and visited with the principal about it. When he chose to ignore the situation, our daughter vandalized the boy's locker. The principal gave her two days' in-school suspension.

Later, the same boy inappropriately touched the principal's daughter. The boy was immediately suspended from school.

This chain of events spoke loudly to our daughter. We spent many hours diligently trying to repair the damage caused by the principal's aloof attitude and inaction.

I also visited school without my daughter's knowledge, demanding a reason for his actions. He leaned

back in his executive chair, raised his arms in the air
and waved his hands back and forth, searching for
words to defend himself. He could not find them.

As I looked at this man before me, my heart filled
with pity. He was the same man who advised me in
high school that the only job I could ever master was
digging ditches. This statement suggested that he
didn't care to understand that my dyslexia wasn't *who*
I was, but a condition I had. "Today," I thought, "he
doesn't care to understand that *foster child* is only a
label for society's ills; it is not a definition of *who*
these children are."

Since I had strong feelings regarding this educated
man who refused to see beyond a learning difference
to know the heart of a kid and who equated foster
children with the plague, a disease, I embraced my
choice philosophy to get past it.

"Even though I can't change this man's behavior
or attitude, I can determine how I will react to it," I
thought. So I dispelled my anger and I refrained from
judgment to focus my attention on our daughter's
recovery.

I knew that Christie and I had to continually walk
a thread-thin line between protecting our children
and becoming an enabler or co-dependent to them.
For this reason, Christie and I never let the children

know when we went to the school or others on their behalf.

However, we never failed to point out that everyone falls short at times because we are all human and teachers are no different. When our children were in the right, we supported them and acknowledged that they did receive inappropriate punishment or treatment from others. Remember, these children lived many years with no one to protect them at all.

In David Pelzer's book, he describes how he wanted his father to be his protector. After his mother stabbed him, he said:

> "I stood before Father in total shock. He didn't even look at me...All my respect for Father was gone. The savior I had imagined for so long was a phony."

This is the magnitude of hurt many foster children experience. So if some of our kids' stories seem trivial or their behaviors seem aggressive to you; remember where they have been. Each and every incident was earthshaking to them. We were the pillars in their lives at this time and we could not, would not forsake them.

Vincent was a senior in high school. He was a

good student and a mature young man. We were and are proud of him. He was making good personal choices and decided to commit fully to whatever he was doing.

So when he went out for sports, he was always at practice. He was always timely, and the team came first to him.

One night on the school bus the kids all became rowdy and guilty of inappropriate travel behavior. The coach caught one young man and banned him from the next track meet.

Vincent went to the coach and explained, "Coach, Doug wasn't the only one acting-out on the bus; there were a lot more of us. He shouldn't have to suffer the consequences alone."

So the coach said: "All of you who were involved in these childish antics stay on the bus when we get home. We need to take care of this."

When the bus reached the school, Vincent and two of his peers stayed on the bus. All other guilty individuals left.

This incident didn't hurt Vincent in the long-run. He was a better person for it.

However, because of the casual intervention by those in authority, Vincent learned he had not escaped the real world.

Instead of taking the time to do the right thing, the coach seemed more interested in getting home and getting out of there. His lack of interest in teaching values gave a free pass to kids who were unable to monitor their own actions and do the right thing for themselves and others.

At home, we tried to teach our kids that truth always renders lighter punishment. This incident taught every kid involved that if you lie, you may get off scot-free.

So we were put to task again, trying to counter this experience by reemphasizing the importance of making personal choices for personal success, regardless of other's decisions. Many parents in America may say, "This is no different than what we have to do every day, too. This isn't an earthshaking experience or all that unusual."

However, our job was not to counter just this one incident, but an entire personal history of negative messages that resurfaced because of it. It can be quite an undertaking. The coach could have changed the outcome by supporting Vincent and his friends in their honesty.

Vincent learned numerous lessons about continuing to do the right thing even when it seemed no one cared. He went out for all the sports and learned many of these lessons on the field, on the court, or on the track.

He was a super bench-warmer for the K-18 baseball team. I kept telling him to keep his head up. "You can't allow yourself to drop your head in self pity," I said. "You must keep your head up so you can identify opportunity when it arrives. It will come, and you can make your mark then."

Vincent stuck it out. He held his head high. Then it was time for the final game of the season. If the team won this game, they would go to State. One of the boys on the team became arrogant and mouthy. The umpire removed him from the game for unsportsmanlike conduct.

Vincent's team was up to bat. It was the final inning. There were two outs; the team was two points behind and two men were on base. The coach put Vincent in to bat.

Vincent hit a strong, low drive to right field. The ball bounced off the outer fence. The two men on base made it home and Vincent was on third base.

The pitcher prepared for the next pitch. He stood on the mound. He breathed deeply. He looked around at Vincent; then he turned to the batter. He threw the ball.

The pitch was low and outside. The catcher missed

the throw and Vincent stole home for the winning run! The crowd went wild.

The team went to State. The young man who was removed from the league game for unsportsmanlike conduct played. Vincent sat the bench. Vincent did the right thing, but again the message he heard was: "It doesn't matter."

When Cody came to live with us, he had just been kicked out of another foster home. This was nothing new for him. He had a tumultuous and lonely history. He had lived in many foster homes. He was also one of the brothers adopted into a home and then dumped back into the system.

Cody knew the phrase 'too bad' well. He had heard it often. Now he was with us. He had no reason to believe this was a good move or that he would remain with us for more than a week or two.

Everyone uses defense strategies and one of Cody's was wry humor. Since wry humor involves irony and may be perceived as sarcasm or mockery, it isn't the best strategy to use in school.

However, Cody did use it often. One day the teacher kicked his desk for a smart-aleck remark, spraying his books several feet across the room.

This behavior didn't surprise Cody. He expected it. He had been surrounded by violence all his life. He had been the object of anger since he was in the cradle. It didn't matter to Cody that the violence was at school and the teacher was free to use it. It was just more of the same.

However, Christie and I were disturbed, but we decided to wait until parent-teacher conference to discuss it with the teacher. Since I knew the teacher well, our conversation began on a personal level.

"I'm sorry to hear your parents got a divorce," I said. "Has it been hard on you? What are you feeling? You know my parents were divorced after I grew up and left the home too. I know it's tough."

"It's been rough," he said. "I'm feeling frustration, anger, disappointment, sadness and a whole mixture of other emotions."

We talked for a little while longer and then I mentioned the incident with Cody. "If you are a grown man," I said, "and you are experiencing all those emotions because your parents got a divorce, how do you think Cody feels? He is only a child and he has been violated, abused, abandoned by his biological parents and abandoned over and over again by strangers. His life has never been stable and he has never had a parent love him or protect him."

Only the teacher knows the real effect of that conversation, but Christie and I were satisfied that we had advocated for a boy who virtually had no voice in the matter.

I have made many mistakes in my life, but one of the biggest mistakes I ever made was in regards to Cody. I told him to write down his feelings on paper. I explained to him and the rest of our kids that expressing themselves on paper would help relieve the hurt. Cody decided to try it. He poured out his heart with vivid description. His words weren't pretty.

They were full of violence and threats. He carried them around with him and stored them in his school locker. Someone found them.

Cody was suspended from school and I drove him to an alternative school in a nearby town. He began to excel there. He made good grades and the school commended him for excellent behavior.

Later he was accepted back into the local community school. He quickly began to fall back into self-doubt and self-denial. He was ultimately kicked out of school when he went to jail.

We didn't adopt Rachel, but she was one of the fifty foster children who lived in our home for a short while. She was beginning to be a 'time-out' kid, spending much of her day in in-school suspension. She couldn't accept the voice of authority.

We tried many things to help her. Finally, we

decided to continue her time-out at home. We began to send her to her room fifteen minutes earlier in the evening if she received a time-out at school that day. After a few days, the teacher came to our home. She said, "You are too hard on Rachel. You need to lighten up."

"Rachel knows that we love her. She always receives a good supper and she is free to move around at will. She needs to know that her decision dictates how she will spend the evening – with the family or without – and that she can change that outcome any time she decides to do it," we answered.

After a lengthy conversation, the teacher agreed that we were the parents, we knew the child best, and we needed to handle it our way. However, we soon learned the teacher had only patronized us. She called social services the next day.

After an investigation, social services agreed with our strategy. The child was loved, fed, safe, and disciplined. They informed the school of the outcome of the investigation. We continued our plan and Rachel soon began to follow school rules.

The teacher's intervention had no merit and just prolonged the process for everyone – especially the child who needed a firm hand to provide structure and security in her otherwise insecure world.

Some people seem to have a need to report foster parents to social services and every time a family is reported, the agency must investigate.

I have thought of a couple of reasons why people may be compelled to do this without reason. (1) Initiating an investigation may make them feel important. (2.) They actually have a personal prejudice toward the child, feel guilty about it, and need to relieve that guilt by doing something noble.

In their minds, initiating a full-blown investigation constitutes noble action. For whatever reason, I think most foster families will attest to the fact that they undergo multiple, ongoing investigations.

Tanner told about his relationship with Cody and their track experiences. The boys were best buddies, shared a room, and were about the same age. Christie and I loved to go to track meets and watch them run.

Coach put Cody in the two-mile run early in the season. He did well, usually placing first or second. Then the coach decided to put Tanner in the same event. In some meets, Tanner would run up behind Cody, but instead of passing him he would slow his pace. He didn't want to pass his brother. We talked about it and I reminded Tanner, "You always need to do your best, Tanner. Talk to each other, encourage each other, but let the best man win."

The boys took me at my word. Soon they were analyzing their racing strategy. Many times the result was a 1-2 man win, coming over the finish line first and second. We encouraged them and cheered them on as a team. It wasn't important who won. It was important that they pulled off a team attitude and a team effort.

Then it was time for the League track meet. The boys were elated. They came to us and said, "Mom, Dad, we're going to take League. We're going to come over the line 1-2 to victory! YES!"

"That sounds great, boys. Mom and I will be there. We'll bring the camcorder and catch you making history. Good job."

The race was exciting. Cody and Tanner paced themselves well. They were in position for the final lap of the race. Their faces revealed intensity. Their strides were free and sure! You could feel their determination! They passed 1-2 over the line. We were all ecstatic!

The boys high-fived; then grabbed hands and started swinging around in a jubilant victory circle. Christie and I were the proudest parents on the stands. What a win! What camaraderie! Our dreams were coming true—but it didn't last.

Joy turned into sadness when the coach walked

onto the field. The boys stopped spinning and stood in silence as he approached them. With a stiff body and grim face, he looked at Cody and said, "You just got your ass kicked!"

Then he walked off the field to wherever pretend coaches walk, leaving Christie and I with his debris. Cody lost all interest in track after that. Nothing we could say could heal the coach's smash hit.

The coach made the race about something different than we planned. I was steaming and had to release the valve. I took the film of the race and played it for the coach and principal. I described a track play-by- play to explain the boy's efforts and goals, pointing out how they had planned, strategized, and succeeded in bringing the school first and second League wins.

I received no apology. Even though there was not a chuckle in the room, I felt laughed out of the office.

Christie's and my principles were our principles only—they would have nothing of it.

I believe coaches need more training on how to empower kids with positive feedback and reward success rather than trash talk for motivation. We were sad the coach was so shallow that he couldn't see the camaraderie between brothers and nurture it instead of kill it.

Cody wasn't our only child who had to attend an alternative school. One of our children became violent, pushing and hitting teachers and attacking Christie and me. The gossip was harsh toward us. Some told us that we were not doing our jobs. They said if we would provide for our foster children, things like this wouldn't happen. It was amazing to us that they discounted the perpetrators' crime and placed blame on the foster parents for the child's dysfunction.

Finally, one evening, I came home to discover toilet paper wadded up in a pile, a thin plastic piece was placed over the toilet paper and a light bulb was on and positioned close to the plastic. By the time I discovered it, the toilet paper was smoldering.

The only one home was this child.

We notified the authorities. The child was placed in a psychiatric medical facility. Within two days the child was diagnosed with Bi-Polar or Manic-Depressive disorder. We were sorry for this diagnosis. Yet, we were immediately relieved. The mystery was solved and we could initiate curative measures. As we thought about the length of time it took us to find help, we realized too much time was lost and too many risks were taken.

All our trips to the medical doctors who told us

that we needed to rethink our child raising philosophy and refused to acknowledge the child had a seri-
ous problem, delayed treatment. All the time we
spent trying to reason with teachers who believed the
child's problem was due to poor parenting, delayed
treatment.

All the days we protected our own family from the
violent episodes culminated the day we found profes-
sionals interested enough to listen and to search for
the problem.

The child spent the next six months in treatment.
In this case, the uninformed opinions of others could
have proven deadly!

This was one of our ongoing problems:

Well-meaning people who helped make matters
worse because they failed to secure all the facts before
moving forward on someone else's behalf.

Those who intervened, without knowing and
sometimes without thinking, were not always casual
acquaintances. Sometimes the interloper was a close
friend or family. One of the most heart-breaking inci-
dents occurred when we were in court finalizing cus-
tody for our granddaughter.

One of our children still struggles with independ-
ence and continues to make poor choices as an adult.
The revelation for change doesn't seem to have mani-

fested itself yet.

However, when the State removed his daughter from the home, he did ask the system to place her with us. So we were in court finalizing this process. To our amazement and without warning our step-mother stood up and addressed the court.

"We think this child should be placed in another home," she said. "You should place the child in a home where none of us know where she is."

We were dumbfounded. Why didn't she come to us with her concerns? We reasoned that she had not been in the family long. She was unaware of the long years of wonderful support and nurturing that her husband and his deceased wife provided. She had come after the fact.

"She doesn't fully understand the scope," we thought. "We will forgive her."

However, after the session, I went to her and said, "Why on earth did you say that? You gave us no inkling that you felt that way. Why didn't you discuss this with us?"

"We prayed about it," she said. "And we thought this is what God told us to do."

"Really," I said. "That is amazing. I have prayed about this for weeks – many times a day! I have asked for guidance and direction - - - - - and God gave me a different answer!"

Christie and I often talked about how much easier our job would be if other people would stop and think before proceeding. Sometimes they interfered as interlopers; sometimes they were simply co-dependents to our children and usurped our authority in that manner.

One of the best examples of co-dependent behavior is when one of our kids convinced a loan institution to give him money when he had no way of repaying it.

I wondered what possessed people with dollar expertise to be swept *under the table* by a $20,000 sob story. Certainly, they had a co-signer, but obviously not a very good one because they eventually came to me for a costly hand-out.

Since I run multiple businesses beside my day job, I owe plenty myself. So when I add $20,000 dollars to the pile, plus interest, I have undertaken a huge debt increase because an institution ran amuck.

I will never forget discussing this state of affairs with the institution spokesperson. The gentleman kept rubbing his temples with his knuckles, making his hair stand straight out. I had to chuckle under my breath.

In view of the situation, the look on this man's

face, and the hair standing straight out from his temples, I thought, "Wow! If I put a plum on the end of his nose, he would look just like Bozo the Clown!"

I guess this thought came into my mind because I thought he had acted like one too.

You are right. I do say, "You can't determine what other people do, but you can determine how you react to it." I guess I was a co-dependent too. I absorbed the debt into my own. Maybe I was a Bozo that day too.

One night the police came to our door. "Mitch is drinking beer on Main Street," he said. "He's standing there with an open bottle and he poked my chest with his pointing finger, taunting me."

"Why are you telling me?" I said. "You were there. He's breaking the law. You're the police. What are you going to do about it?"

"You know, Harvey, sometimes you just need to be the parent and leave the law up to the law. You need to go get him, bring him home, and take care of him."

"No, you need to help him understand consequences and do your job," I retorted. "You need to enforce the law. Otherwise, nothing matters!"

The police returned to Main Street and gave Mitch a citation for a minor in possession of alcohol.

However, the next evening he took three boys and a girl home in an intoxicated condition and no citations.

Alcohol was no stranger to Mitch. He struggled with it on a daily basis. His system just couldn't tolerate the drug. The night his friends brought him home in a drunken stupor, I knew immediately this was not a simple, usual drunken episode.

I knew time was crucial. "Don't take him out of the car here!" I yelled. "Get him to the hospital *NOW.*"

This was the last straw for us. We were extremely concerned over the teen alcohol consumption in our community. I visited three churches to ask if they would join me in setting up a drug testing program. All declined getting involved, saying they feared their participation would result in a decrease in church membership.

Personally, I believe every bottle of alcohol should have a bar code on it with an identifying number. The person who buys the beer or other alcoholic beverage should have to sign when purchasing it, connecting them to that particular bottle. If the bottle is found in a teen's possession, the buyer could be identified.

The law would need to enforce the law so there

could be several places for snags even using this system.

As crisis after crisis plagued our household, people began coming to us and voicing their opinions. My boss came to me and said, "You need to send those kids back. The cost to your medical insurance for your child's extended stay in a mental ward guarantees you won't get a raise for the next five years!"

The local attorney also gave us a warning, "You need to send those kids back where they came from. You are no match for them. You are in way over your heads."

Even my mother said, "Delbert, you need to give up the kids. They are going to break you emotionally, financially, and spiritually. I am worried about you, son. I'm sorry; you are the most important one to me!"

"We can't, Mom," I answered. "We are all they have or have ever had. We can see now why their struggles are so profound. Even when someone will take them and love them, the rest of the world wants to bury them. We have given our word to support them. We will not go back on that word. We will be here for them regardless . . . ."

Things did get rough for Christie and me many times. One day one of our foster children became

angry when we were out golfing. Balls and clubs
began to fly; profanities poured out loud and clear.

Since I was afraid someone might be injured and I
wasn't sure what would come next, I placed the child
in a hold. However, this time something went awry. I
broke the child's thumb in the process.

This was almost the final deal for me. Guilt was
eating me up. I was ready to quit. "Everyone is right,"
I thought. "What do I think I am doing anyway? I
guess I am in over my head. I have no expertise for
this. Yes, the kids will break me emotionally."

I almost forgot my motto: *You can't determine what
happens to you; you can only determine how you will
react to it.* I prayed and I prayed and I prayed.

The next morning Christie called from our flower
shop downtown. "Delbert, you need to come to the
shop. Someone wants to see you."

"Really," I said. "Who is it?"

"I'm not going to tell you. It's a surprise."

I went to the shop. When I reached the door, I
could see her through the glass. It was Rachel. She
was standing there with two little girls at her side.
"Well, my goodness," I said. "What do we have here?
It is so great to see you."

Rachel introduced Christie and me to her twin
daughters, and we visited for a long while. Then an

amazing thing happened. The teacher who had told us that we were too hard on Rachel - the person who reported us to social services - walked into the shop. I believe the timing was divinely orchestrated because this teacher had never been in our store.

Rachel was talking and she continued as the teacher stood there and listened. "You know," Rachel said. "I want to thank you so much! You not only saved my life, but you saved my little girls' lives too.

Sometimes when I feel on edge and need to calm down, I think of you. I sit in my overstuffed chair, grasp the arms of the chair tightly, and pretend you are holding me in a pin position. I imagine your strength. I feel your care. I remember all the time that you dedicated to me. Thank you from the bottom of my heart!"

I was awestruck! My prayers were answered at that moment. God was telling me what I must do through the messenger before me. Stick in there. Fight the fight. Do what has to be done. Love.

"You have no idea," I said, "what you have just done for me. I thank you from the bottom of *my* heart."

Then I explained that her story had just given me a reason to continue. We laughed and the women may have cried.

I didn't cry, but my heart was bleeding for her and all the other children in America who are forced to travel that road to maturity."

The ongoing family crises, our confrontations with community and school authorities, and our fight against teen drinking and drug use resulted in unexpected ramifications. My job was not only in jeopardy, but virtually gone before I realized it.

I had worked for the company for over twenty years. The General Manager was about to retire. I was a likely candidate for the position.

I had worked in almost every facet of the company through the years. I knew each department well. I had assisted and worked closely with the acting General Manager.

However, our company's board president, with a select few employees and community members, began a back-biting strategy to keep me from securing the position. They cited *'my baggage'* as a reason for not hiring me.

Actually, this was the grand finale because my baggage had disturbed more people than I knew. An active campaign to dismiss me from my job had begun many months earlier.

It seemed ironic to me that the man who eagerly carried a petition against me was also the first person to teach me a lesson about fraud.

When I was a teen, I baled hay for this man. We agreed that my payment would be one-third of the bales. When I went to the field to haul my bales home, the field was empty! He had taken all of them. I never did receive pay for my work.

Now this gentleman was carrying a petition to oust me from the General Manager competition, citing my baggage as the reason that I was not qualified.

It took me awhile to understand what my baggage was. I heard rumors that my children were my baggage. However, that didn't really make any sense to me because this gentleman also had an adopted child. However, his child never went the foster-home route. She was a newborn baby when they got her.

Most of our kids had already lived life before we came along. Only Rashona was adopted at birth. The other kids came to us when they were in grade school or junior high school. They had already been deeply injured. Maybe he thought that made the difference.

Later a new company was buying our company out and I learned the baggage story was not a rumor. It was the truth. An executive from the new company came to me and said, "Your seven adopted children were identified as *your baggage*. They are the reason that you were black-balled from the position. It is all legal because it was not formal. It was all under the rug kind of stuff."

Since I believe in conducting honest business deals and strive to communicate in a forthright manner, I have a terrible time understanding the thought processes of these people.

I ask myself how people broadcast untruth as truth and never flinch in the process. What makes these people tick?"

We lived in a small town and this information was whispered from doorway to doorway. Our children heard it, knew it, and absorbed it. I knew what it was doing to Christie and me, but I couldn't even imagine how it might be affecting them. Our children had become the culprits again without even being there. They couldn't escape it.

Even though this episode was extremely difficult for our entire family, we did escape further damage due to the excellent thinking of my existing supervisor.

Personnel in the new company wanted me to help sample grain for protein content before the buy-out. My supervisor went head to head with them on the matter saying, "Delbert is not going to help sample. That is the end of it."

I had kept close tabs on all grain in our inventory

and knew the grain was superior quality. However, as we expected, the report on their grain samples indicated the grain was inferior.

If it was true that the grain was inferior, it would have resulted in a loss of thousands of dollars to our existing company in the buy-out. We pulled our own samples and had the grain tested again.

Our sample reports indicated the grain was superior quality. If I had helped with the first sample as the new company requested, they could have given me credit for taking good grain samples. I would have become the scapegoat that dearly cost the home-company and community.

This did provide a new twist to our story, however, because the General Manager of the new company later cited a new reason for my departure.

He said, "If you had not disobeyed my order to sample the grain for testing, you would still have a job."

"Wow," I thought. "He has a poor memory. He forgot about my baggage and he also forgot that the argument about grain sampling was between him and my acting supervisor. I was out of the loop."

The incident made me reflect on some of the hard times - times when it would have been easy to throw in the towel. I thought about when Christie went to school so we could open the flower shop and two of our kids were in jail, and I was barely making it at home with the rest of the kids.

However, I knew then what I know now. So I said, "God is protecting my family. I love my wife and every one of our children without reserve. I must push forward for Christie's sake, for the kids' sake, and for my sake. My example in this horrible situation is a mega-phone in my children's ears – we must make the choice to forgive and overcome."

And then I said, "With the Lord's help, we will!"

Chapter 6

God's Revelations

"Dad," Vincent said, "I got it. I got the promotion! I'm going to be overseeing up to thirty people now. The raise isn't bad either. Isn't it great?"

God's timing is perfect, pristine, wonderful, without blemish! I didn't get the General Manager's job, but Vincent did get his promotion.

"Thank you, Lord," I said. "It isn't about me. It's about you and what we can do for you."

"That is great, Vincent. Thanks for calling us and letting us know."

"Well," Vincent said. "How is it with you dad? Is everything okay?"

"Let me tell *you*, some wonderful news too, Son. After things went totally sour with the home company and I was forced to walk out the doors for the last time, something amazing happened.

Exactly a minute and a half after my feet hit the pavement, my cell phone rang. It was great news. Another company wanted to hire me.

They offered me a tremendous opportunity. I accepted. Everything is good here. Thanks for asking."

There were so many people committed to reaching out to our family. When Mitch returned home after spending time in jail, a local company hired him on the spot.

"I could see your passion and vision," the owner told me. "I wanted to do something to be a part of it. What actually happened is I was the one rewarded. Mitch is a great young man. He is talented and doesn't need to be told anything. Just point him in a direction, and he takes care of the rest!"

Cody also landed a good job. One gentleman that I had known for years came to me. He said, "You know that I am working with Cody now, don't you? I have wanted to do something for you because you helped me so much. You may not know it, but you helped me become a better person. You also helped save my marriage. Now I know how I can repay you."

"You don't owe me anything," I said. "You deserve everything you have. You became who you are today because of whom you are."

"No," he said. "I want to nurture your son and support him just like you did me. That won't be hard to do either because he is a super-good worker. He is great to have around. He is going to go places in this world."

Sometimes the goodness of people can be as overwhelming as the trying times. It makes a person swell up inside and see God face to face.

When scripture talks about Moses being unable to look into the face of God because of His brilliance, I understand. At times like this, one wants to fall face down in His presence.

All the good things happening to Vincent made my mind go back in time. I remembered the hard times. I remembered when he fought with teachers and students and us. I remembered the times I held him tightly in a hold and talked and talked.

Then I remember the changes – the understanding look, the helpful behavior, the concern for others. When I remember the night of his high school graduation, a lump builds in my throat, my face becomes flushed and warm, and I can't keep the tears from streaming down my face.

"Vincent Harvey," the principal called as he presented the graduating honors.

Vincent stood. He walked, proud and tall, to the stage. He was a man now in every right. He was strong and able. He had overcome.

When he reached the stage, the principal smiled warmly, shook Vincent's hand and said, "Vincent, we are proud of you! You have received the United States of America Purple Heart Award for high school students. This award is given to you in honor of your academic excellence, leadership role, and participation in school and community affairs. We salute you for this endeavor. Congratulations!"

I know that I was not the only one crying. I actually heard other muffled sounds in the room. It is amazing how the turn-around success of others has the ability to humble so many of us.

Our children have blessed us in so many ways. Vincent's Purple Heart was just one of them. When I think of the real reason we started taking in foster children, I have to think about all my mother's prayers and Christie's family and her time in church.

My mother prayed continuously for me to accept Christ as my Savior and specifically prayed for me to become a man who would help pull others out of the ditch. I could never have partnered with Christie to serve these foster children without my mother's prayers and God's intervention and guidance. Christie's deep dedication to her children was an inspiration to me.

When times became really rough, God's impeccable timing reminded me that He was still with us and that He was still in control. I was visiting with a gentleman one day when Cody was in jail.

I had been asking myself so many questions about how we could have helped Cody better. I was pretty depressed that Cody might be in jail for a couple of years instead of months. Then this gentleman walked into my office and sat down.

The man didn't come to me for grain prices or protein content or other business. He liked Cody and wanted to check up on him. So he stopped by to see me. "You know I really like ol' Cody," he said. "What is he doing now?"

"He is in prison," I answered. "We thought we were doing everything we could for him. I have been wondering though, what we could have done differently to help change this outcome."

The man stood up. He was a tall man. His majestic stature dwarfed me when I was standing. So I felt like a dot on the paper as he looked down at me sitting at my desk. He spoke with emphasis in his strong, deep voice, "Don't pine," he said. "Your son still has a chance. My son shot himself at eighteen!"

The jolt was immense. This man's presence and statement brought me back to reality. Cody did have a chance. He was still breathing, thinking, and reacting. He wasn't dead.

I finally rested in the fact that Cody had to make the difference. We couldn't do it for him. No matter how much we cared, no matter how much we loved, Cody had to make the *choice* to turn his life around. We needed to be there for him, but we couldn't do it for him.

Then one day the phone call came. Cody was out of jail and was coming home to try to make it. He came home and accepted the job with the local company with a built-in mentor to-boot. Cody was getting his second chance at life.

Our family was maturing, growing and beginning to be on the up side of down. It was getting easier to discount the naysayers like the person who told us we were *'crazy folks down the road.'*

"You need to watch it," he said. "Those kids will bite you, spit on you, scratch you and devour you. Then they will walk out of your life and never turn around to know what you've tried to do for them!"

I wrote about people with that mindset in the last

chapter. It is fantastic that our book continues with healing and hope. It is fantastic that we can say, "Nope, you were wrong this time and this time and this time."

It's not about us. It is about Him and the children He has given us to serve!

Machi is another young man on the way up. Even though Machi cried when his brothers descended into depravity, he followed in their footsteps for awhile. He also discounted what is right and became familiar with the inside of a jail cell.

As with the prodigal son in the Bible, we, too, opened our arms to him on his return home. The same company that hired Mitch responded in kind for Machi. So the brothers are both working for the same company. The owners are caring individuals who extend their words into action. They don't just talk about their faith; they live it.

I have talked about the three brothers and their return to good decisions. Tanner must be mentioned here too. Even though he was born to me, he has an equally profound story to tell.

Tanner could have had his Dad all to himself. He could have enjoyed one-on-one fishing trips, cattle drives, movies, or whatever he wanted. Yet, he ended up sharing his Dad with over fifty other siblings. That is a lot to ask of a kid.

Also, Tanner was right to say that some of those passing through our home brought the poison with them – the poison of the perpetrator's vice. When children are removed from their horrid surroundings, everything doesn't just stop. It follows them until they can make sense of the world. They must learn that they are truly free from it and can now choose their own direction.

If I am fortunate enough to leave anything when I pass on, Tanner must share that inheritance with seven adopted siblings. Without siblings, he would have had it all.

These are just a few things that Tanner dealt with as a youngster. There are many more. So it is not surprising that he also went through a difficult time. However, the day Tanner called and said, "Dad, I'm ready to go to school now," was one of the happiest days in my life. I was jubilant about his decision. I couldn't wait to help him get started.

Tanner went to school, obtained a managerial position and will be starting a new journey in business soon.

He is a chip off the old block and I can't stop talking about his talent and the mature decisions he has made.

Sometimes when we talk about our blessings and we tell stories about our kids' successes, we feel we neglect to tell enough wonderful stories about Mitch. Maybe it is because he is a quiet kind of guy. He doesn't expect or demand much fanfare. He is who he is and he is satisfied with that.

God has blessed Mitch with such talent. He was barely in high school or maybe just junior high when we were talking one day. I said, "You know what Mitch? It would be great to have a hutch in that corner. I think I'll invite a builder in someday to do that for me."

I was assigned to go on a three-day business trip so I left the next morning. When I returned, there was a new beautiful corner cabinet in our home. Mitch had built it to surprise Christie and me.

Mitch is the unassuming man over there in the back of the room. He is compassionate and caring. He made sure his siblings had plenty to eat when they were small children, and he still looks after them today. He opens his home to them and assists in every way he can.

We saw God in our lives in so many ways. We knew and understood many of the graces he poured upon us, but some were beyond our understanding.

One example is the tornado that went through our

community. The twister circled around town causing extensive damage to several homes.

During the heat of the controversy over the General Manager's position, one gentleman told me that he wanted to *'run me out of town on a rail.'* He was aggressive and almost out of control when he spoke to me. This person and the person who called my children 'baggage' were thorns in my side.

If I gave anyone the impression that I think I'm perfect, forget that! I was aching to confront both of these gentlemen and had already approached the board president. I said, "If I find that your actions have hurt any of my kids, I will personally come back and be in your face big time."

However, that all changed after the tornado. The tornado set down, damaged several homes, skipped around the community to the west and then damaged homes on the north. It stayed on the ground much of this time. We looked out and saw it within feet of our own door, but it didn't do any damage on our property.

Ironically, two of the homes that did receive extensive damage were the homes of the people I had planned to confront. I shook my head in disbelief. I knew it wasn't my style to hit someone when he is down. I never went back.

I decided to put my energy into helping change the prospects for foster children all over America. I wanted to write a book, develop a song to catch people's attention, and set up a *Fund of Choice* to serve young people all over America who were raised in foster homes, who had been adopted, or those from broken homes.

I asked Vincent to work on words for a song. "Dad," he said, "I don't know anything about music. I wouldn't be a good one to do that."

"Vince," I said. "Any time you are in doubt, anytime you question your ability, ask the Lord – the Man upstairs. He will guide you."

Everyone seemed to question this one aspect of my dream until Vincent met up with a casual acquaintance. He told Vince that his dog was lost.

"I've been looking all over for him," he said. "Someone told me they saw a dog with his description on a street back off Main Street. I'm going over in that area to look for him. Want to come along?"

"Sure," Vincent said.

As they searched, they continued to talk. "You know, Vincent, you're a lucky guy."

"Really?" Vincent asked. "What makes me lucky?"

"I was a foster kid like you. Did you know that?" he asked.

Then he continued without waiting for an answer, "I was a foster kid like you. The only difference is you were placed in a good home. I wasn't. I wasn't placed anywhere at all. It was a rough go. I've put my feelings in a song. I'd like to play it for you sometime."

Vincent was awestruck. "Dad," he told me later, "chills ran up my back when he told me he had written a song about foster kids. At that moment I got it. I'm with you now. I understand what you want to do."

Our experiences taught us many things, but one of the most important lessons we learned is that the goodness of some people makes all the poor choices and shortsightedness of others obsolete –unimportant.

The poor choices of one or two principals were obliterated by the great counsel and affirmative action of other school officials. When our child diagnosed with Bi-Polar was expelled for hitting and attacking teachers, the acting superintendent worked diligently to arrange opportunity in a second-chance school for this youngster.

These stories are just a small example of how God intervened in such wonderful ways. When we were down, he brought angels to our rescue. When we were about to give up, he gave us signs to continue.

When we wanted to strike back, he calmed our spirits. When our resources were almost depleted, he refilled the reservoir.

Even though most of our children are raised and the only one left in our home is Rashona, we are determined—with God's help— to continue serving these deserving young people throughout our great nation. Our goals are huge and far-reaching, but I know with Him we can make it!

Chapter 7

Outside of Self

"Wow!" My mother shared with Christie and me, "I had a real eye opener when I started working for the department store. Many of us are spoiled and into ourselves in this country. I don't think some of us realize that it takes all of us to *make it work*.

"I find adult clothes rolled up in a wad and stuffed beneath the children's display counter, women's clothes crumpled in a corner under the seat in the boy's fitting room, and appliance boxes opened and parts left everywhere.

"I also find clothes all over the fitting room floors, plastic hangers stepped on and broken, and underwear bags opened with one of three pairs missing.

"I actually heard one mother tell her children, 'It's okay if we trash it; they hire people to pick up after us.'

"I often hear parents tell their children to go play with the toys while they shop. Then we find torn books and pick up toys ripped out of the packages and broken. I had no idea we had descended into this mindset. I was shocked!"

"Yes," I said. "It's sad that we are the richest nation in the world, but some of us would rather destroy that wealth rather than use it for good."

This conversation may seem like a bummer after the last chapter because America is full of wonderful committed people who want to make a difference.

However, stories like this must be told because we can't climb to the summit unless we gauge where we currently are. We can't accomplish wonders if we refuse to look at reality. Our world is not all 'warm and fuzzy' and anyone thinking of foster care or adoption must realize that.

Christie and I are like millions of other Americans who could have taken another route. We could have raised one son, taken exotic trips all over the world, forfeited what we believed in to climb the work and social ladder, and said, "Let the perpetrator burn in the hot spot and his kid with him. The whole thing will be generational anyway!"

However, we didn't live our lives like that and we have brothers and sisters all over America who believe like we do and have spent their lives helping to *make it work.*

To eliminate the foster system back-log, we need a community focus and an interrelated system that empowers the foster and adoptive parents and gives support and encouragement to the kids.

Schools must be committed to understanding and developing strategies to work with abused children just as they have with children with learning differences.

Providing structure and support to the parents of these children are of utmost importance. The learning process for the child who has been through the foster system must be a team effort just as it is with any other exceptionality.

Most children, in foster homes or in homes with their natural parents, will play parent against parent to get what they want. They will do the same with the teachers and their parents if allowed to do it. So what a positive impact it would make on any child if she knew her parents and the school were on the same page and were working for the same outcome.

Churches should be alert to the blended families in their communities. In recent years, divorce care classes have emerged in many churches throughout the country, helping divorced adults and their children restructure their lives for success. Certainly, the abused child is no different. Bible classes and blended family support should be the order of the day.

In a booklet called *Day After Tomorrow* the author discusses how important it is to allow a child with learning differences to be a child. She urges us to not to blame everything the child does on to his learning difference.

This is also true with the abused child. We need to remember that no matter how worldly he has become, how crusty he might seem, somewhere deep down inside him, he is still a child.

As he begins to grow in his new environment and begins to let his armor slide, he will still do what all children do. Sometimes that is appropriate and pretty and sometimes that is inappropriate and not so pretty, but it is part of the natural growing process.

Another cardinal rule when working with abused children is to refrain from equating any of their poor choices or bad behavior with that of the perpetrators – their biological parents. If anything is known about a successful biological relative, they may be an example for the child. However, making the child feel guilty for his parent's crimes is inexcusable and will only serve as a catalyst for bad or violent behavior.

I'm not trying to be a counselor here. I'm not one, but Christie and I have had experiences with over fifty foster children in the past twenty years.

We know what worked and what didn't work.

We know what the kids have told us and we have heard the reflections of more than a dozen grown foster kids on an intimate level. So we are attempting to share with you our story, and the kid's first-hand experiences in many different homes.

I talked earlier about the foster care agencies saying that you don't have to be wealthy to be foster parents. You don't have to be perfect either. No one is perfect. We all fail, sometimes miserably, but our hearts need to be in the right place – extended to the children and their ultimate welfare. We have to take children into our homes for the right reasons.

Children are adept at spotting insincerity. They know when a person is genuine. When Cody said foster and adopted children were like used cars –some are okay, most are lemons and discarded - he said that because it became his experience as he left foster home after foster home.

Our heavenly Father is Truth, but in our relationships with each other we must contend with perceived truth daily. Maybe the foster parents who adopted Cody and his brothers could explain their actions. Maybe their hearts were in the right place. We can't judge that.

However, Cody's perceived truth – the message he internalized – was he was like a *thing* to be discarded when someone was through with him.

We need to work with the social services agencies to help them become better, more efficient. They are not brokers. They are *service agencies*, working with live little people with hearts that have already been broken. Some practices like advertising children on television or on the radio should be prohibited. These children are not cattle or cars or toys on a shelf. They are children who are violated when they are advertised and no one comes to get them!

Every second from the time a child is removed from her biological home should be invested in the her welfare by the foster care agencies, the schools, the churches, the foster parents, adoptive parents, children's organizational groups, the community. The only way this can happen is through education. It is our guess that many people believe that once the child is removed from a bad situation, all is well. That could not be farther from the truth. That is actually the point when everything begins to happen.

One child described the experience of being removed from her home as being 'aborted' later in life rather than taken from her mother's body before birth. This is a graphic description, but, again, it is the perceived truth for the child.

Even though the child may hate her abusive existence, it is all she knows. It is her norm no matter how bad the situation is. When she is removed from the home, the norm is gone; everything is unknown. She has been ripped from history, sometimes from siblings, and maybe a grandparent who was the only staple in her life.

It takes time and energy to meet new expectations, understand the reasons, and build a new norm. The child needs all of us outside of ourselves and working together.

It is our experience when these children begin to understand and evolve into the persons God meant them to be, they are grateful that they were removed from the home. As Vincent put it, "I am not only appreciative, grateful, and thankful, I will be indebted to them for the rest of my life!"

For each of our children who made that conscious decision to change his or her life, they experienced an 'aha moment.' We call it a moment, but the realization actually manifests itself over time.

They begin to realize that the past is the past. They can relive that past by making it a part of their lives today or they can choose to move in another direction, wiping out failure and making success generational. When they understand their power of choice their life takes on new meaning, new direction, and they become the people God intended them to be.

Chapter 8

For the Love of Him

God is the Father of choice. He planned it; He designed it; and He created it. He gives you and me *free will*, the choice to invite Him into our lives. So why do we think it is surprising that every decision we make here on earth also involves choice?

According to Christian Statistics online, there are 224,457,000 Christians in the United States. Since we make the choice to pick up our cross and follow Him when we invite Him into our hearts and receive the Fruit of the Spirit, why are there 127,000 children being passed from house to house because no one wants to commit to them?

To break down this thought, let's engage in a few *'what if'* scenarios just for the fun of it.

When we count all 224,457,000 Christians, just one family out of 1,771 families could dissipate the foster system back-log in this country.

However, since the number of documented Christians includes children, the elderly, and those who are disabled or unable to care for others, let's cut the number for possible adoptive homes way down.

One-fourth of the 224 million represents a little over 56 million people. If we use this greatly reduced number to cite the same type statistics, it would still take only one in every 439 families to solve the foster care problem.

Simple math tells us that we only need 127,000 homes to adopt all the children in the foster care system. So why have we discussed the round-about numbers? There are two reasons for this. (1.) One hundred twenty-seven thousand seems like a huge number until we compare it to 56 million potential homes. This comparison reduces the 127,000 to size. The new numbers have changed our perspectives. So we are more likely to ask: "Why do we have children needing homes at all?" (2.) The round-about numbers also provide a snapshot view of the number of people available to assist families who do decide to bring a child into their home. As we talked earlier, it takes the whole community to minister to these children. There are teachers, scout leaders, coaches, youth directors, tutors, music instructors, and dozens of other child-serving professions in the remaining 168 million people.

We need these families too. Their input and support are crucial for overcoming community prejudice, for ending the abusive cycle, for supporting the adoptive families and for helping nurture the adopted child!

Some may want to use our family as a reason not to adopt a child. They may say, "If they had that many problems, I can't do it. I'm not up to it."

Yes, all adoption does require love, patience, and emptying oneself, but remember our family is not the usual. We didn't adopt one child; we adopted seven children! Also, only one of our children was adopted at birth, coming to our home straight from the hospital. Six of our children had traveled the abuse, ship-to-nowhere route and three of them were deemed unadoptable by the system before we invited them into our home. We knew this information before we made the choice to increase our family by seven.

We have a profound belief that the family is what will sustain America. By saving these children, we are investing in another human being, helping cut the generational cycle of abuse to the quick, and contributing to a strong America. Wow! What wonderful rewards for loving, enjoying, and appreciating a tiny bundle of potentiality – a child.

To be very truthful with you, we could not have made it through the tough times without the Holy Spirit to guide us.

Jesus said, *"But the Counselor, the Holy Spirit, who the Father will send in my name, will teach you all things and will remind you of everything I have said to you."* John Chapter 14, verse 26.

The Holy Spirit offers us a gift - the Fruit of the Spirit. Galatians 5, 22-23 explains: *"But the fruit of the Spirit are love, joy, peace, patience, kindness, goodness, faithfulness, gentleness and self-control. Against such things there is no law."*

These divine gifts are the answer to living. This joy is not dependent upon worldly affairs and allows me to get up in the morning and truly say, "I'm superb today," even when I have three sons in jail or I'm driving a child to alternative school, or someone has disappointed me for the umpteenth time.

God has not only given me the option to choose, but He has given me so many options. He has given me a way out!

First Corinthians 10:13 helps me know that I can love rather than hate. I can support rather than abandon. I can forgive rather than blame and I can focus on my blessings rather than my hardships. When I weaken, He carries me.

"No temptation has seized you except what is common to man. And God is faithful; he will not let you be tempted beyond what you can bear. But when you are tempted, he will also provide a way out so that you can stand up under it."

The final sign that I was to write this book came to me when we met with one of our fifty foster children after about nine years. When we opened our door and saw Jake standing there, we were thrilled. We invited him in and visited for a long while.

"Jake, I said, "I have about completed a book that I'm narrating. Is there anything that you would like to say about your experiences as a foster child?"

"Yes," he said. "You know how much the kids liked to tease me. To my peers, I guess I was the pin-up cartoon kid. It was tough. When I was in your home, I had support. If I summed up the most important thing I learned, I would say – I learned respect."

At this moment, I am focusing on me and Christie because so many people ask, "How did you do it?" One of our deacons put it this way, "Man," he said, "I couldn't have an iron stomach like you do!"

"It isn't about the stomach," I answered. "It's about soul-searching every day to focus on what is important - then having the courage to follow your heart."

I always continue to say that it isn't about us. It's about 127,000 mini-Americans who need a family, who need a cheer, who need someone to care:

- *Will we wake up and see?*

      There are so many 'little people' in our midst who are struggling to survive, struggling to maintain, struggling to make sense of an insensible world.

      Will we put down our hammer and nails and step away from our computer keyboards so we can experience what they feel?

      Will their loneliness and pain muster us to the call or will we turn our heads and forget it all?

- *Will we wake up and see?*

      There are so many 'little people' who have grown tall and strong. They have made it against all odds.

They aren't someone because of
you or me. They are who they were
meant to be.

They surveyed all their choices
and honed in on the good ones.

They're making new histories for
you and me, themselves, and their families.

• *Will we wake up and see?*

When we take one little life to
love and mold, it becomes reciprocal. It
filters down through the generations.

When our children are loved, their
children are loved and their children
are loved also.

It is so great to see our children
and the grandchildren building a new
legacy. It helps us know that choices
were everything they were meant to be.

These bullets may seem a little poetic for the
rough and tumble, but they soften the hard truth. As
for Christie and me, we have made our choices. We
want to continue to give to these deserving young
Americans, helping those who made the choice to

make a new history.

We have established a *Fund of Choice* non-profit organization to provide start-up money or other financial assistance to individuals who were in foster care, who were adopted, or who were from broken homes. Designated proceeds from the sale of this book will help provide funds for this organization.

Now it is time for *America* to make a choice – an America with over 224 million residing Christians.

How marvelous it would be if 127,000 would chose to mentor, love, and accept a child and the remaining 220 million would assist and support them and their children. With God's grace we can do it and with God's grace we will do it!

"Only You Can Control You"
by
Tanesha Harvey
8 years old

A child's concept can sometimes be a great teacher for all of us. Tanesha wanted to share her view about *It's All About Choice!*

To purchase the *It's All About Choice Book*

To donate to the Fund of Choice Organization

or

To schedule a speaking engagement

Contact us at:

Delbert Harvey

Quinter, Kansas 67752

785-754-2301

or

785-754-8233

delbert@choiceisit.com

Bibliography

Christian Statistics, "The Largest Christian Populations,"
http://www.adherents.com/largecom/com_Christian.html

Foster Care Alumni of America,
http://www.fostercarealumni.org/resouces/HR6307.html

Holy Bible. *New International Version* online @
http://www.ibsstl.org/niv/index.php

Pelzer, Dave. *A Child Called It.* Dear Beach, Florida: Health
Communications, Inc., 1995